The Power of Video Technology in International Comparative Research in Education

Board on International Comparative Studies in Education

Monica Ulewicz and Alexandra Beatty, *Editors*

Board on Testing and Assessment
Center for Education
Division of Behavioral and Social Sciences and Education
National Research Council

NATIONAL ACADEMY PRESS
Washington, D.C.

NATIONAL ACADEMY PRESS • 2101 Constitution Avenue, N.W. • Washington, D.C. 20418

NOTICE: The project that is the subject of this report was approved by the Governing Board of the National Research Council, whose members are drawn from the councils of the National Academy of Sciences, the National Academy of Engineering, and the Institute of Medicine. The members of the committee responsible for the report were chosen for their special competences and with regard for appropriate balance.

This study was supported by Grant No. REC-9815157 between the National Academy of Sciences and the U.S. National Science Foundation. Any opinions, findings, conclusions, or recommendations expressed in this publication are those of the author(s) and do not necessarily reflect the views of the organizations or agencies that provided support for the project.

International Standard Book Number 0-309-07567-X

Additional copies of this report are available from National Academy Press, 2101 Constitution Avenue, N.W., Lockbox 285, Washington, D.C. 20055; (800) 624-6242 or (202) 334-3313 (in the Washington metropolitan area); Internet, http://www.nap.edu

Suggested citation: National Research Council. (2001). *The power of video technology in international comparative research in education.* Board on International Comparative Studies in Education, Monica Ulewicz and Alexandra Beatty, Editors. Board on Testing and Assessment, Center for Education, Division of Behavioral and Social Sciences and Education. Washington, D.C.: National Academy Press.

Printed in the United States of America

Copyright 2001 by the National Academy of Sciences. All rights reserved.

THE NATIONAL ACADEMIES

National Academy of Sciences
National Academy of Engineering
Institute of Medicine
National Research Council

The **National Academy of Sciences** is a private, nonprofit, self-perpetuating society of distinguished scholars engaged in scientific and engineering research, dedicated to the furtherance of science and technology and to their use for the general welfare. Upon the authority of the charter granted to it by the Congress in 1863, the Academy has a mandate that requires it to advise the federal government on scientific and technical matters. Dr. Bruce M. Alberts is president of the National Academy of Sciences.

The **National Academy of Engineering** was established in 1964, under the charter of the National Academy of Sciences, as a parallel organization of outstanding engineers. It is autonomous in its administration and in the selection of its members, sharing with the National Academy of Sciences the responsibility for advising the federal government. The National Academy of Engineering also sponsors engineering programs aimed at meeting national needs, encourages education and research, and recognizes the superior achievements of engineers. Dr. William A. Wulf is president of the National Academy of Engineering.

The **Institute of Medicine** was established in 1970 by the National Academy of Sciences to secure the services of eminent members of appropriate professions in the examination of policy matters pertaining to the health of the public. The Institute acts under the responsibility given to the National Academy of Sciences by its congressional charter to be an adviser to the federal government and, upon its own initiative, to identify issues of medical care, research, and education. Dr. Kenneth I. Shine is president of the Institute of Medicine.

The **National Research Council** was organized by the National Academy of Sciences in 1916 to associate the broad community of science and technology with the Academy's purposes of furthering knowledge and advising the federal government. Functioning in accordance with general policies determined by the Academy, the Council has become the principal operating agency of both the National Academy of Sciences and the National Academy of Engineering in providing services to the government, the public, and the scientific and engineering communities. The Council is administered jointly by both Academies and the Institute of Medicine. Dr. Bruce M. Alberts and Dr. William A. Wulf are chairman and vice chairman, respectively, of the National Research Council.

BOARD ON INTERNATIONAL COMPARATIVE STUDIES IN EDUCATION

Andrew C. Porter *(Chair)*, Wisconsin Center for Educational Research, School of Education, University of Wisconsin, Madison

Gordon M. Ambach *(ex officio)*, Council of Chief State School Officers, Washington, D.C.

David C. Berliner, College of Education, Arizona State University

Christopher T. Cross, Council for Basic Education, Washington, D.C.

Clea Fernandez, Teachers College, Columbia University

Adam Gamoran, Departments of Sociology and Educational Policy Studies, University of Wisconsin, Madison

Manuel Gomez-Rodriguez, Resource Center for Science and Engineering, University of Puerto Rico, Rio Piedras

Jeremy Kilpatrick, Department of Mathematics Education, University of Georgia

Marlaine E. Lockheed, World Bank, Washington, D.C.

Lynn W. Paine, Department of Teacher Education, Michigan State University

Janet Ward Schofield, Learning Research and Development Center, University of Pittsburgh

Warren Simmons, Annenberg Institute for School Reform, Brown University

Joseph Tobin, College of Education, University of Hawaii

Colette Chabbott, *Director*
Monica Ulewicz, *Program Officer*
Jane Phillips, *Senior Project Assistant*

BOARD ON TESTING AND ASSESSMENT

Eva L. Baker *(Chair)*, The Center for the Study of Evaluation, University of California, Los Angeles
Lorraine McDonnell *(Vice Chair)*, Departments of Political Science and Education, University of California, Santa Barbara
Lauress L. Wise *(Vice Chair)*, Human Resources Research Organization, Alexandria, Virginia
Richard C. Atkinson, President, University of California
Christopher F. Edley, Jr., Harvard Law School
Ronald Ferguson, John F. Kennedy School of Public Policy, Harvard University
Milton D. Hakel, Department of Psychology, Bowling Green State University
Robert M. Hauser, Institute for Research on Poverty, Center for Demography, University of Wisconsin, Madison
Paul W. Holland, Educational Testing Service, Princeton, New Jersey
Daniel M. Koretz, RAND Corporation, Arlington, Virginia
Richard J. Light, Graduate School of Education and John F. Kennedy School of Government, Harvard University
Barbara Means, SRI International, Menlo Park, California
Andrew C. Porter, Wisconsin Center for Education Research, University of Wisconsin, Madison
Loretta A. Shepard, School of Education, University of Colorado, Boulder
Catherine E. Snow, Graduate School of Education, Harvard University
William L. Taylor, Attorney at Law, Washington, D.C.
William T. Trent, Department of Educational Policy Studies, University of Illinois, Urbana-Champaign
Guadalupe M. Valdes, School of Education, Stanford University
Vicki Vandaveer, The Vandaveer Group, Inc., Houston, Texas
Kenneth I. Wolpin, Department of Economics, University of Pennsylvania

Pasquale J. DeVito, *Director*
Lisa D. Alston, *Administrative Associate*

Preface

The Board on International Comparative Studies in Education (BICSE) was established by the National Research Council (NRC) in 1988 at the request of the U.S. Department of Education's National Center for Education Statistics (NCES) and the U.S. National Science Foundation (NSF). Under its initial mandate, the board monitored U.S. participation in large-scale international comparative studies. Beginning in 1998, BICSE expanded its charge to include synthesis, analysis, and strategic planning for international comparative education research and synthesis of lessons learned from past and current studies.

The Third International Mathematics and Science Study (TIMSS) has been the focus of much of BICSE's agenda in the 1990s. BICSE has monitored each phase of TIMSS and has explored methodological issues raised by the study. Though it was not the first comparative study to make use of video technology, the TIMSS Videotape Classroom Study represented one of the innovative dimensions of TIMSS's ambitious design, and it captured the attention of the U.S. education community.

Video technology has been an important methodological tool for inquiry in classroom research for more than 40 years, and it has also been used in other international comparative research on a more limited basis. However, TIMSS triggered a great deal of enthusiasm for the use of video technology in educational research because it was the most comprehensive effort to measure student achievement ever undertaken. In addition, the TIMSS Videotape Classroom Study led to advances in digitizing video data that have revolutionized the use of this technology in education research. Consequently, both the enthusiasm about the TIMSS Videotape Classroom Study and the technical advances resulting from it have increased general interest in international video studies among education researchers and policy makers.

In response to this interest, BICSE hosted a 1-day workshop in November 1999 to explore three issues: the potential that video technology appears to offer as a tool to enhance and expand international comparative research, the role of international video in informing educational research and professional development in the United States, and the methodological questions raised by the use of this research tool. The workshop brought together a diverse group of scholars, drawing on decades of experience with video technology, from educational anthropology, psychology, teacher education, and international comparative education. The workshop discussions provided a great deal of information and stimulating ideas for the board's deliberations, which focused on the unique possibilities and challenges presented by *international* video. Our recommendations are intended to guide researchers and policy makers interested in international comparative education and in the use of video technology as a powerful methodological tool.

The board owes a particular debt of gratitude to the eight leading scholars who contributed substantively to the success of the workshop: Frederick Erickson, John Frederiksen, Drew Gitomer, Ricki Goldman-Segall, James Hiebert, Catherine Lewis, Heidi Ross, and James Stigler (see the Appendix for their affiliations). These scholars provided insightful written reflections on questions framed by the board and took the lead in the rich discussions that ensued. The board also extends sincere thanks to Magdalene Lampert and Ray McDermott for contributing their expertise to the workshop as discussion leaders.

On behalf of the board, I extend sincere gratitude to a number of people whose help was invaluable in this undertaking. Board members Clea Fernandez, Lynn Paine, and Janet Schofield took the lead in conceptualizing, planning, and synthesizing the workshop discussions. Another board member, David Berliner, was invaluable in providing support throughout the process and leading discussions. Joseph Tobin, who has subsequently joined the board, played a key role in the workshop, first by serving as a discussion leader and later by contributing to the writing of this report. Several NRC staff members deserve recognition: Patricia Morison for her leadership in guiding the board from the earliest stages of the workshop planning through the drafting of this report; Alix Beatty, for her extensive contributions to the planning of the workshop and the writing of the report; and Jane Phillips, for her able administrative support. I extend thanks to Colette Chabbott for her leadership in the later stages of the report writing phase and to Monica Ulewicz for finalizing the report. I thank Eugenia Grohman for her expert editorial advice and Kirsten Sampson Snyder for her guidance of the report through the review and production process. Thanks are also due to our sponsors at NCES and NSF for their support during the planning of the workshop, in particular Eugene Owen at NCES and Larry Suter at NSF, who have been great friends of BICSE's work for many years.

I also thank all my fellow board members for their insightful contributions to the workshop discussions and the deliberations that led to this report. Their thoughtful consideration of methodological issues in international comparative education throughout the year has been influential in the shaping of this project.

This report has been reviewed in draft form by individuals chosen for their diverse perspectives and technical expertise, in accordance with procedures approved by the Report Review Committee of the NRC. The purpose of this independent review is to provide candid and critical comments that will assist the institution in making the published report as sound as possible and to ensure that the report meets institutional standards for objectivity, evidence, and responsiveness to the study charge. The review comments and draft manuscript remain confidential to protect the integrity of the deliberative process. We thank the following individuals for their participation in the review of this report: Ronald Gallimore, University of California, Los Angeles; Herbert Ginsburg, Columbia University; Kenji Hakuta, Stanford University; Ramsay Selden, American Institutes for Research; Reed Stevens, University of Washington; and Daniel Suthers, University of Hawaii at Manoa.

Although the reviewers listed above have provided many constructive comments and suggestions, they were not asked to endorse the conclusions or recommendations nor did they see the final draft of the report before its release. The review of this report was overseen by Marshall Smith, Stanford University and the William and Flora Hewlett Foundation. Appointed by the National Research Council, he was responsible for making certain that an independent examination of this report was carried out in accordance with institutional procedures and that all review comments were carefully considered. Responsibility for the final content of this report rests entirely with the authoring panel and the institution.

Andrew C. Porter, *Chair*
Board on International Comparative
Studies in Education

Contents

Executive Summary	1
Introduction	3
Brief Historical Perspective on International Video Research	4

Power of an Image
    Is It Too Powerful?, 10
    How Important Is Contextual Information?, 11
	8

Integrating Qualitative and Quantitative Analysis	12
Sample Size	14
What Video Can and Cannot Capture	16
Privacy and Confidentiality	18
Professional Development	20
Links Between Achievement and Teaching Practices	23
Conclusions and Recommendations	24
References	26
Appendix: Workshop Agenda and Participants	29

EXECUTIVE SUMMARY

Video technology has evolved into a powerful methodological tool for international comparative research in education. It provides a lens through which to view and record classroom practices. International video studies generate data that can create audiovisual glossaries of teaching strategies and skills that expand the repertoire of possible teaching approaches. This audiovisual glossary provides a reference point for teaching practices that are difficult to describe in words, particularly when foreign languages and cultural contexts create barriers to interpretation and communication. Carefully selected videotapes can introduce teachers to a variety of practices, to help them to rethink what they might otherwise take for granted, to consider the pros and cons of different approaches, and, in general, to become more reflective practitioners.

International videotapes serve as a record of teaching in a particular time and place, and make that teaching available for multiple reexaminations; they facilitate collaboration among researchers from diverse perspectives that traditional forms of data collection limit in cross-national studies. Recent advances in storing and coding large volumes of footage permit researchers to move quickly through digitized videotapes for specific events or words. Ancillary data, such as teacher questionnaires and student work, can be stored with videotaped footage to augment the video data with contextually rich background data. Coded video data can help track the myriad interactions within a classroom, such as the amount of time spent in teacher-student interactions. Quantitative analysis of coded images may clarify broad trends and variations, and qualitative analysis can facilitate deeper understanding of quantitative phenomena, such as how teacher-student interactions take place. Archived video data can be reexamined in the future by researchers with new research questions.

Video technology offers a number of important potential benefits to researchers and policy makers interested in international comparative research. However, a number of practical and methodological issues remain to be addressed, including sample sizes and the confidentiality of research participants. In light of the potential benefits and recognizing the unresolved issues, the Board on International Comparative Studies in Education (BICSE) offers four recommendations to researchers, funding agencies, and policy makers.

Recommendation 1: The international comparative education research community should pursue projects that appropriately use video technology as a research tool.

Such research will help scholars build a body of work that can contribute fundamental new understandings of educational practices, while at the same time resolving some of the important methodological challenges discussed in this report.

Recommendation 2: The international comparative education research community should support not only large-scale studies that make use of video technology, such as the Third International Mathematics and Science Study (TIMSS), but also other kinds of video-based research.

Research studies with a variety of sizes, goals, and methodologies can benefit from the application of video technology in important ways that have the potential to stimulate progress in both methodological and substantive issues.

Recommendation 3: The international comparative education research community should undertake initiatives, such as the support of a working group, to help clarify and develop solutions to the privacy and confidentiality issues in using video technology in such research.

The very nature of video technology creates problems for and challenges to confidentiality that cannot be easily handled by simple extrapolation from existing procedures for other research methods. Thus, serious and focused consideration of confidentiality issues in video research, especially in international settings, is needed to develop creative solutions and to foster discussion and consensus building around such solutions.

Recommendation 4: The international comparative education research community should undertake initiatives, such as the support of a working group, to explore the creation of a video archive or archives for international comparative research in education.

Video technology can be of significant benefit in expanding the accessibility and application of comparative research and in serving as a unique historical resource. Given the substantial costs associated with both international comparative education research and video technology, wide distribution and archiving will contribute to its cost effectiveness.

INTRODUCTION

Throughout the history of educational research, scholars have used a variety of methods to study classroom interaction in order to analyze the complexities of teaching and learning—ethnographic case studies, interviews, and questionnaires to analyze content, pedagogical strategies, classroom cultures, and teacher-student interactions. More recently, the potential contribution of film and video technologies have expanded the repertoire of tools to provide rich qualitative and quantitative data for analysis of classroom environments (Bogdan and Biklen, 1992; Jordan and Henderson, 1995; Stigler, Gallimore, and Hiebert, 2000). As the technology advances rapidly, however, scholars must confront fundamental issues about both its possibilities and limitations in educational research.

The Board on International Comparative Studies in Education (BICSE) held a workshop to consider the benefits and complexities of using video technology in comparative education research. Participants included scholars with expertise in contemporary ethnography, teacher education, cognitive science, international comparative education, and videography in educational research and teacher professional development (see the Appendix for the workshop agenda and participants).

BICSE invited several participants to write brief responses to the following set of targeted questions on the use of video technology in comparative educational research and professional development:

- What are the strongest arguments for and against the use of video technology in international comparative studies of education?
- If you were asked to advise the planners of such a study, what recommendations would you make about its design? How should it be conducted? How should results be analyzed and disseminated? How would you address methodological issues, such as the ethics of the data collection and handling?
- What particular challenges or opportunities would conducting such a study internationally pose?
- Can you point to studies—not necessarily comparative or large-scale ones—that might inform our thinking about the use of video technology?

Responses to these questions served as a starting point for a day-long discussion of the advantages, barriers, and possible future directions for the use of video technology in international comparative research.

BICSE structured the workshop around three particular uses of video technology. One discussion focused on the use of videotapes to systematically collect and aggregate images of classrooms in order to record and portray trends or patterns of classroom practice across different countries. A second discussion explored the use of videotaped images to support the professional development of teachers to improve classroom practice. The third discussion considered efforts to link the variation in teaching practices captured on videotape to achievement differences identified within and across countries.

The workshop discussions clearly illustrated that video technology has evolved into a powerful tool for use in international comparative education research. The workshop also generated rich discussions of a variety of both methodological and analytical questions that relate to the role video technology can play in such research.[1]

Over the course of several meetings, the board explored further the issues raised during the workshop to synthesize lessons learned from the international comparative studies using video as a methodology. The board developed several conclusions and recommendations for researchers and policy makers regarding the use of video in future international comparative education research. This report presents highlights from the workshop discussions and from the subsequent board work on this topic; it is intended to provide an overview of the issues, not to provide specific methodological procedures for using international video.

Video in international comparative research in education has lately received a great deal of attention, most notably in light of the public release of the TIMSS Videotape Classroom Study. The use of video in educational research has been evolving in many fields, from anthropology to qualitative research traditions in education, ethnomethodology, sociolinguistics, and interactional analyses.[2] The next section provides an overview of the historical context of video in international comparative research and therefore highlights selected works from international perspectives.[3]

BRIEF HISTORICAL PERSPECTIVE ON INTERNATIONAL VIDEO RESEARCH

Video technology is emerging as an important ethnographic research tool in the fields of educational anthropology and psychology. Ethnographers use a variety of methods to describe and interpret "events that occur within the life of a group, with special regard to the social structures and the behavior of the individuals with respect to their group membership . . . and the meaning of these for the culture of the group" (Taft, 1985:1729). Early fieldwork required researchers to observe and interview participants, to take copious notes during or

---

[1]Many issues raised in this workshop, such as the relationship between cross-cultural versus within culture studies, have been fundamental to comparative and cross-cultural research for many years (see, e.g., Campbell, 1961).

[2]For more detailed analysis of these qualitative traditions, see Erickson (1986, 1992), Jordan and Henderson (1995), and McDermott and Roth (1978).

[3]The workshop and board deliberations did not include discussions on the history of video in international comparative research. The board has added this overview as useful background for the reader.

after the observations, and to translate their findings into written accounts. Cameras enabled ethnographers to expand their data collection efforts to record real-time images for subsequent detailed analysis (Henley, 1998).

Anthropologists Margaret Mead and Gregory Bateson were pioneers in the use of film for ethnographic research. They first used cameras—both still and motion picture—in their work in Bali in 1936-1938. They used film to record "the types of non-verbal behavior for which there existed neither vocabulary nor conceptualized methods of observation" (de Brigard, 1995:26). For 2 years, Mead and Bateson lived in the mountains at Bajoeng Gede, filming and photographing family life in villages.

> We tried to use the still and the moving picture cameras to get a record of Balinese behavior, and this is a very different matter from the preparation of a "documentary" film or photographs. We tried to shoot what happened normally and spontaneously, rather than to decide upon the norms and then get the Balinese to go through these behaviors in suitable lighting (de Brigard, 1995:27).

Mead and Bateson later spent 6 months collecting comparative data among the Iatmul in New Guinea. From the 25,000 still photographs and hundreds of hours of film footage, they prepared *Balinese Character* and edited several films in the Character Formation in Different Cultures Series for cross-cultural comparisons of behavior patterns, as in *Bathing Babies in Three Cultures* (de Brigard, 1995; Bateson and Mead, 1952). Mead and Bateson's innovative use of film technology in Bali has been described as "by far the most significant ethnographic research use of visual media in the first half of this century" (Henley, 1998:44).

Mead's work in early childhood development was a precursor to the field of educational anthropology, which emerged in the middle of the twentieth century (Spindler and Spindler, 1992). Leading educational anthropologists such as George and Louise Spindler focused their ethnographic research on classrooms as cultural contexts. Their comparative work in two schools (in Schoenhausen, Germany and in Roseville, Wisconsin) was a groundbreaking use of video technology as both a means to collect cross-cultural classroom data and as "evocative stimuli" for later discussion about cultural differences (Spindler and Spindler, 1992). This long-range study examined the influence of culture on the role of the school in the preparation of children for an urbanizing environment and changing world. The Spindlers aimed to capture a more complete record of activities in the classrooms, playgrounds, and on field trips than had previously been possible.

> We filmed in Schoenhausen and in Roseville, and we showed the teachers, children, and administrators the films from both places. We conducted interviews about what they saw in their own classrooms and in those of the "other" and how they interpreted what they saw (Spindler and Spindler, 1992:80).

The Spindlers coined the term "cultural screens" to describe the way viewers interpreted the images they saw of school life.

In describing their research in Schoenhausen and Roseville, the Spindlers explained that the "greatest utility of films as 'records' is that we can 'return' to the classroom years later" (Spindler and Spindler, 1992:78). They described how reexamining the images recorded from 1977 to 1985 revealed new insights.

> One phenomenon, for example, that came to our attention through repeated viewings of the films was that despite great variations in the explicit aspects of teacher style in the management of classroom activity, all of the teachers in the Schoenhausen school were in constant charge of their classrooms. . . . Although they might take a position in the back or along the side of the room and seemingly be quite relaxed about what was going on, we saw that teachers were giving signals, sometimes as subtle as pursed lips or raised eyebrows, to reinforce or intervene in student behavior (Spindler and Spindler, 1992:78).

The Spindlers described the value of recorded images to educational anthropologists in terms of two important issues: archiving data for secondary analysis at a later time and stimulating reflective thinking by viewers. The use of film and video technology has enriched qualitative descriptions of school environments as cultural contexts; see Box 1.

By the end of the 1980s, researchers were looking for a way to integrate the qualitative richness of small-scale video studies with the representative sampling of large-scale quantitative approaches in cross-national studies. The TIMSS Videotape Classroom Study provided such an opportunity. TIMSS was one of a series of mathematics and science achievement studies conducted under the auspices of the International Association for the Evaluation of Educational Achievement. TIMSS tested and gathered contextual data from students in 45 countries at three age levels. Funded by the National Center for Education Statistics (NCES) of the U.S. Department of Education, the TIMSS Videotape Classroom Study had the goal of clarifying some of the contextual factors that might help explain differences in achievement. TIMSS was the "first large-scale study to collect videotaped records of classroom instruction in the mathematics classrooms in different countries" and the first "to attempt observation of instructional practices in a nationally representative sample of students within the United States" (Stigler et al., 1999:2).

The TIMSS Videotape Classroom Study drew from a randomly selected subsample of German, Japanese, and U.S. eighth-grade mathematics classrooms already participating in TIMSS; it used a national probability sample from each of the three countries to create a comparative picture of eighth-grade mathematics teaching. In the United States, researchers also planned to examine the effects of reform policies on U.S. mathematics teaching practices (Stigler, Gallimore, and Hiebert, 2000). The work on the TIMSS Videotape Classroom Study

> **BOX 1**
> **Using Videotapes as Cues for Reflective Thinking**
>
> In the Preschool in Three Cultures Project, Joseph Tobin, David Wu, and Dana Davidson (1989) used video technology as a tool for analyzing the cultural meanings of preschool in Japan, China, and the United States. In their study, videotapes were used not as data, but as cues for reflection. Tobin, Wu, and Davidson videotaped days in one preschool in each culture and then edited the tapes down to 20 minutes. These videotapes became cues for interviews they conducted with the classroom teachers. They showed the teachers the videotape of their classroom and asked them to explain the thinking behind their actions. To address the question of typicality, they showed the videotapes to teachers, administrators, and parents associated with six other preschools in each country, asking them to describe their reactions to the practices on the videotape. Another feature of their method is that they asked informants in Japan, China, and the United States to comment on the videotapes made in all three countries. This method produced understanding of some very interesting findings, including, for example: Japanese teachers' tendency to hold back from intervening in children's disputes; Chinese teachers correcting the over-indulgence that single children receive at home; and American teachers teaching young children to express their feelings in words.

led to important breakthroughs that have earned video studies a new place in international comparative studies.

The techniques developed for digitizing and coding marked a major advance in the use of video technology as a research tool. Researchers found that combining quantitative and qualitative analyses allowed a more comprehensive examination of classroom practice across cultures. "Quantitative coding is necessary to validate insights gained from close qualitative analysis. . . . . On the other hand, qualitative descriptions are essential because they lend substance and coherence to the results of quantitative coding" (Stigler, Gallimore, and Hiebert, 2000:95).

Research in video ethnography continues to stimulate new technology in the storing, coding, and sharing of video images. Ricki Goldman-Segall, at the Multimedia Ethnographic Research Lab (MERLin) at the University of British Columbia, has been developing tools for video analysis and annotation on the Internet. "Web Constellations is the first server-side, Web-based database system designed to enable a community of researchers to catalog, describe, and meaningfully organize data accessible on the Web" (Goldman-Segall, 1998:145). Using this technology, Goldman-Segall has posted videotaped data on the Internet from her comparative study of computer cultures. In the study, Goldman-Segall used video technology to examine the influence of computers on elementary and middle school students' understanding of their own thinking as they explore science. Her web site allows visitors to view the video images and to discuss the nature of teaching and learning through on-line communication. Goldman-Segall's work exemplifies the rapid innovations in video technology in the last decade and its influence on ethnography as a research tool.

International video technology offers a number of important potential benefits to scholars, practitioners, and policy makers interested in educational research and practice. It also raises a number of practical and methodological issues about the early planning stages of video research. This section of the report describes the primary benefits of—and caveats associated with—using video technology in international comparative studies in education.

POWER OF AN IMAGE

Early in the workshop discussions, participants focused on a topic that seems almost self-evident: the compelling nature of visual images themselves is the prime advantage of video technology. James Hiebert, Catherine Lewis, and Frederick Erickson helped workshop participants explore some of the reasons video images are so powerful and the uses and misuses of that power. All three agreed that videotapes capture more of what happens in a classroom than do other forms of data collection, such as self-reported data from teachers collected through interviews or questionnaires. Erickson explained that the difficulty in collecting valid data on classroom practice from teachers is that no teacher can take in the myriad interactions in his or her classes: "[Teachers] can only report very globally their recollections about the 'how' of classroom practice." Erickson asserted that the video record serves as a "resource for the illustration of instructional and learning behaviors through an audiovisual real-time record of the real-time enactment of those behaviors."

Videotaped images provide both a lens through which to view classrooms and a tool to develop a shared language with which observers can discuss what they see. Of particular importance is the value of this shared language in building a common professional language of teaching. The problem of defining "good" teaching is extremely complex, but the difficulty of finding words to refer to a specific aspect of teaching and being perfectly understood exacerbates the problem. Video technology, especially video from another country, with a mix of familiar and unfamiliar practices, heightens the possibilities of providing fresh insights. By providing an audiovisual record of countless teaching approaches, international video studies provide an audiovisual glossary of teaching tools, strategies, skills, styles, pitfalls, and mistakes. For example, a conversation in which a teacher's videotaped actions can be freeze-framed and viewed repeatedly can help to establish some common understandings about and terms to describe classroom practices. Such a common professional language of teaching would be very useful to both practitioners and researchers in minimizing linguistic differences in describing observed behaviors and focusing instead on significant classroom practice; see Box 2.

Such an addition to the discourse has specific benefits for cross-cultural and cross-national work. The practical problem of describing classroom instruction in words is further exacerbated when these interactions take place in a foreign language and an unfamiliar culture. While videotape does not eliminate the need for translation and discussion of a classroom's cultural context, visual images provide a reference point that can make cross-cultural differences and similarities more readily apparent. James Hiebert offered an example from the TIMSS-Repeat (TIMSS-R) Video Study. TIMSS-R was conducted in 1999 to measure the mathematics and science achievement of eighth-grade students (ages 13 and 14) and to measure trends in mathematics and science achievement in countries that participated in TIMSS.

The TIMSS-R Video Study videotaped national samples of mathematics and science teaching in seven countries. Research collaborators from the participating countries met to develop a coding scheme to interpret the teaching practices in the videos and to compare practices across countries. The international group developed a coding scheme to analyze four dimensions of classroom instruction compa-

---

BOX 2
Developing Shared Language of Practice Through Video Analysis

In Learning from Mentors, a comparative study conducted through the National Center for Research on Teacher Learning, Lynn Paine and colleagues examine mentoring practices for novice teachers in China, the United Kingdom, and the United States, and how novice learning is shaped by institutional and social contexts. Videotaped lessons and mentoring sessions in one site are shared with mentors in each of the other sites. The results of using this process have proven useful in unexpected ways. One videotape that showed a Shanghai beginning elementary teacher teaching a lesson and then debriefing with her mentor afterward drew vehement responses from the majority of U.S. mentors. The U.S. mentoring teachers voiced criticism about the seemingly intrusive approach used in China to show a novice teacher how to teach particular content. Discussion about the video sessions stimulated the U.S. mentors to examine their own assumptions about mentoring practices, which they had not been able to clearly articulate to researchers in initial data collection.

Analysis of concrete and unfamiliar practices captured on video helped researchers and mentors create a common understanding about theretofore vague generalities, such as mentors playing the role as "guides" and their efforts to "support" novices' learning. The use of video technology for discussion about mentoring stimulated mentors to examine what they really meant by guidance and support and how they believed such guidance and support are best provided. The chance to examine practices concretely, but to do so at some distance from one's own practice, afforded both participants and researchers insights into unexamined assumptions about learning to teach.

rable across countries: content, actions of participants, discourse, and climate. Hiebert highlighted an example from a German-speaking community in Switzerland, where some mathematics lessons are devoted to an activity eventually labeled "working through." Prior to the video study, the nature of this activity had been difficult to translate. By looking at how the four dimensions were coded and comparing them to lesson activities in other countries, however, the research group eventually came to a common understanding of "working through." Hiebert explains: "Video data permit researchers from many countries to collaborate around concrete examples of classroom processes and to sort out superficial and linguistic differences from significant classroom practice differences."

This example also illustrates another point that several workshop participants emphasized: the importance of truly collaborative interaction between international partners. Video technology creates an opportunity for researchers from diverse perspectives to examine and interpret concrete examples of teaching behaviors in a way that is typically not possible through more traditional forms of data collection in cross-national or comparative research. This type of collaboration can enhance communication among researchers about different methods of video analysis. Several workshop participants expanded this point: the research community needs to actively create international participation in every phase of a study to avoid a single nation-centered perspective. As Hiebert and others noted, each member of an international research team should be considered a valuable resource and be committed to sharing the meanings they make of videos from their country and other countries.

A second potential advantage of video technology in international and cross-cultural research is that videotapes allow viewers to witness a volume and variety of classroom lessons that may not be possible any other way, and to see them in juxtapositions that can generate valuable insights. For example, depending on the nature of the material that has been archived, a researcher can, in the span of a day or a month and without leaving home, become immersed in the elementary mathematics teaching of classrooms thousands of miles away. Alternatively, the researcher could examine treatments of a particular concept, age level, or other element across numerous countries. For U.S. researchers, policy makers, and educators, these external reference points allow for deeper insights into U.S. teaching practices, both in terms of providing new ideas and in creating greater clarity about their own practices. Hiebert maintains that video allows U.S. educators to "[h]old a mirror alongside contrasting pictures from other countries to see our own practice more clearly; [and] uncover concrete examples of alternative practices not imagined within our own culture."

Is It Too Powerful?

The convenience with which videotapes can be shared and reviewed, however remarkable, relates to what has been perhaps the most prevalent concern expressed about video research. Viewing even one videotaped lesson is a very powerful experience, sometimes deceptively so. Seeing one—or ten—mathematics lessons in Japanese classrooms cannot transform an observer into an expert on teaching in Japan, but it may make him or her feel like one. An observer who did not already have considerable understanding of Japanese culture and the structure of education in Japan could easily make unfounded and possibly incorrect inferences about the lessons, the teachers, the students and what they learned, the schools, and many other things. Joseph Tobin referred to this exaggerated sense of confidence about what observers think that they know about a classroom after they have observed only a few videotapes as the "problem of video seduction or verisimilitude." Tobin pointed out that as a society "we are gullible watchers of video," that audiences have a tendency to give themselves over to the authority of the researchers and their video data. Heidi Ross illustrated this point in her description of a colleague's interpretation of the TIMSS Videotape Classroom Study:

> [The TIMSS videotape] confirmed everything he believes he knows about why many American students fear and are not generally high achievers in mathematics. . . . . The vivid and seemingly bounded lessons [that videotapes] convey can easily obscure the complexity of teaching and learning contexts, and be used to solidify, rather than open to sensitive investigation, previously held assumptions about learning and teaching.

Erickson also noted that relatively little research has explored people's perceptions of videotapes or, indeed, of other means of recorded events, such as written narratives or field notes. Addressing the problem of overgeneralization remains a major issue in broadening the use of video technology.

How Important Is Contextual Information?

The compelling nature of video images also raises another question: Can videotapes stand alone as data, independent of any contextual information? Erickson argued that the videos record behavior but not the meaning behind that behavior. Information about meaning lies in understanding the thought processes that the teacher uses (Erickson, 1986). For this reason, David Berliner and others argued that to make sense of videotaped images requires contextual information. "I learned very quickly that, unless I understood the purposes of teachers, I really didn't understand the behavior I was coding," Berliner noted. The significance of contextual information becomes greater in international video research in which data are collected about unfamiliar practices and cultural meanings are less well known and not explicit.

Catherine Lewis agreed that collecting a variety of data to supplement videotapes is crucial:

Because of video, classroom practice may come to life to a much greater extent than other aspects of the educational system—for example, textbooks, standards, working conditions, management practices. To the extent that classroom practice is a product of all these factors, there arises a danger of overattributing causality to the classroom, because it is easily grasped and memorable, in contrast to other systemic factors, which may be murky and yet causative. This could lead to too much focus on teachers in change efforts, without adequate grasp of the other system factors that may be pulling classroom practice back to a particular norm within a country.

Many workshop participants favored collecting a wide variety of ancillary data to augment videotapes. Teacher interviews before or after the recorded lessons can capture teachers' goals for and their reactions to the taped lessons. Questionnaires can gather background data on the students, the composition of the class and the school, the teacher's goals and qualifications, and the administrative structure of the school. Student work can demonstrate assessment and learning outcomes. Workshop participants noted that the low cost of computer memory and improved scanning techniques mean that a wide range of ancillary data could be stored and searched in connection with videotapes. Such supplementary information about the context in which a lesson takes place can reduce the gaps in time, space, and culture between the researchers who use the tapes and the events they are trying to understand.

In contrast, James Hiebert argued for using videotapes independent of other data, depending on the research questions being asked. He suggested that if a researcher is studying the nature of mathematical explanations and how teachers in different countries explain fractions, for example, analysis of videotaped footage in and of itself could provide the needed information. The researcher might not need additional contextual information about—for example, cultural perceptions about mathematics in that country—to understand what is happening in the video. Hiebert said: "There are things that you can learn from watching video. . . . Our problem is that we do not yet know what the bounds of those things are." He cautioned that the difficulty lies in identifying the limits to what can be gleaned from video data. Hiebert advocated exploring the limits of this methodology, while at the same time recognizing that images can stand alone as data for certain purposes.

INTEGRATING QUALITATIVE AND QUANTITATIVE ANALYSIS

Scholars of education as well as others interested in their findings have often been frustrated in their efforts to bridge the gap between qualitative research that explores and describes the behavior of students and teachers and quantitative research on educational phenomena. Workshop participants discussed the potential of video for integrating qualitative and quantitative analysis. Several noted that the challenge of reconciling qualitative and quantitative research is particularly salient in international comparative work, where the combination of different cultural contexts and different methodologies makes it especially difficult to bring potentially complementary perspectives together. Coding videotapes can help researchers track data, such as the frequency of particular classroom events or the relative amount of time spent in teacher lecture, teacher-student interactions, group work, and individual work. Quantitative analysis of coded images of events may clarify broad trends and variations.

Suppose, for example, qualitative analysis of videotapes from classroom lessons in Australia reveals a highly effective questioning technique used by the teacher. From this one classroom, generalizations about teaching practices in Australia could not be drawn, but the observation could become a hypothesis to be tested quantitatively with a large sample of coded videotaped classrooms in Australia. Alternatively, quantitative analysis of videotaped images could be supplemented by qualitative investigation. For example, qualitative analysis of classroom culture might reveal insights about the social context conducive to cooperative learning. Researchers could analyze videotaped lessons in Japan and the United States to examine how dimensions of social development, such as willingness and capacity to express disagreement respectfully, influence group dynamics in classroom settings (Linn et al., 2000).

Coded video data may help to explore the generalizability of some qualitative findings, and qualitative data may help to illuminate the meaning of quantitative coding of videos. But challenges remain, particularly with coding. As described in the previous section, contextualizing recorded behavior is important in understanding the meaning behind that behavior, and it is especially important when coding across cultures (Erickson, 1986). Similar behaviors in different cultures may have very different meanings, and comparisons can be problematic. Stigler and colleagues (1999) describe the methods they used in developing coding procedures for the TIMSS Videotape Classroom Study to gain an accurate portrayal of instruction in Germany, Japan, and the United States. For example, their field test brought together a team of six code developers (two from each country) to watch and discuss the contents of pilot videos ". . . to develop a deep understanding of how teachers construct and implement lessons in each country" (Stigler et al., 1999:23). This collaborative process led to the generation of hypotheses about what the key cross-cultural differences might be, and these hypotheses formed the basis of the codes to quantitatively describe the study videos. Coders for the main study trained with the field test videos, and a formal reliability assessment was conducted across coders to ensure agreement. This coding procedure demonstrates how researchers are developing methods to address the questions of coding reliability in cross-cultural comparisons. Improving video coding and analysis techniques to determine precisely what might constitute a trend, a significant variation, or typical practice in a given context are issues that remain to be explored.

SAMPLE SIZE

Sampling and variability present methodological challenges in large-scale, cross-national research. These same challenges arise in international video research, and are related to the issues of generalizability and the power of videotapes noted above. Seeing a handful of videotaped lessons does not qualify one as an expert on the teaching style of a particular country. But how many taped lessons might one need in order to reach a conclusion about a particular point about a particular teacher or about the teaching of algebra in a country as a whole? How does cross-national variation in teaching practices relate to student achievement? To speak with confidence about cross-national comparisons, is it necessary to videotape a national probability sample in each country in a study?

Adam Gamoran used the TIMSS Videotape Classroom Study to illustrate this issue. In the videotapes of Japanese classrooms, students worked on mathematics problems before they were given the formula; the videotapes of U.S. classrooms show students first learned the formula and then worked on problems. Can one conclude anything about the two countries from these observations? Gamoran argues that examining the variability in these practices *within* countries would help in understanding achievement differences:

> If that practice were completely homogeneous within countries, then we could never learn whether that practice was associated with achievement differences since, as Jim Stigler points out, we have an *n* of three at the country level in the TIMSS Video Study. So we need to know more about variability within countries in practices like that, just as a starting point for ultimately bringing a focus on relating classroom practice to student outcomes.

Other scholars also note that within-country variation can be as great or greater than cross-national variation, and that it is not yet possible to control for major socioeconomic, racial, and ethnic factors that affect teaching and learning. This point is addressed in BICSE's report, *Next Steps for TIMSS* (National Research Council, 1999). As in any cross-national research, political structures and cultural characteristics play a major role in explaining variation in education. Catherine Lewis noted: "I think it [within-country variation] is one more source of data, but it doesn't get us out of the problems of cross-national comparisons with all the things that vary across nations."

How then might researchers select a sample that allows investigation of variations in practices? Hiebert noted that the primary research questions in the TIMSS and TIMSS-R video studies related to teaching within and across countries. Yet the budget only allowed one lesson per teacher to be taped. "This, in turn, meant that little can be said about the nature or quality of individual teachers or about how lessons are sequenced. An obvious alternative would be to tape two or three lessons in sequence for each teacher, but then fewer teachers would be taped and the national representativeness would be lost," he said.

To assess the reliability of video observations from the TIMSS Videotape Classroom Study, Stigler and colleagues asked teachers, after the videotaping, to evaluate whether their videotaped lesson was typical (Stigler et al., 1999). The researchers were concerned that the presence of the video camera might have altered classroom instruction and reduced the validity of the study. Teachers were asked to rate their level of nervousness and how the lesson they taught for the videotaping fit in a larger sequence of lessons. On the basis of teachers' self-reports, the researchers concluded that the TIMSS Videotape Classroom Study captured a fairly representative sample of what typically happens in eighth-grade mathematics classrooms in Germany, Japan, and the United States (Stigler et al., 1999).

Sampling and variability are related to real-world questions about the reasons for undertaking the research, the intended uses of the data, the funds available to support it, and the interests of those who provide the funds. International video research is expensive in comparison with more traditional methods of classroom research, and efforts to ensure that the research design avoids the potential pitfalls mentioned above only increase the expense. For example, is it sufficient to videotape only the teachers, or must one see the students' reactions and interactions in order to understand the lesson? Are videotapes of single lessons from teachers sufficient, or are videotapes from multiple lessons necessary to capture valid information about a teacher's practice?

While board members are sensitive to the many ways video research might be improved, we conclude that the importance of particular improvements varies with the purpose for which the research was being conducted. As Hiebert explained, a nationally representative sample was chosen for the TIMSS and TIMSS-R video studies because the primary research questions focused on teaching within and across nations, rather than teachers or classrooms. Large-scale video studies such as TIMSS and TIMSS-R have great potential value in providing reliable and valid cross-national descriptions of teaching behavior. For example, Stigler noted that increasing the number of countries in the video study would make it possible to say more about the relationship of teaching and learning at the country level (though not at the teacher level). He indicated that the TIMSS-R Video Study has increased the number of participating countries to seven, including more high-achieving countries and one lower-achieving country. The researchers expect this sampling design will allow them to investigate, at the national level, some features that high-achieving classrooms might share. For other large-scale video studies, the criteria guiding the selection of participating countries might include a range of educational governance systems, a range of cultures, and other macrolevel factors. For these kinds of purposes, the sample of countries need not be large. Moreover, although it may well be important to conduct such research on a regular basis, the necessary interval between studies might be quite long.

Other more modest and inexpensive methods of classroom studies have value as well, of course. Case studies and experimental investigations of more focused questions can be used in a variety of ways and might well be done more frequently and on a less regular schedule than large-scale studies. Research on Japanese science lessons by Linn and colleagues (2000) provides an example of one such study. To explore the divergence in science performance between U.S. and Japanese students between fourth and seventh grade revealed in TIMSS, the researchers used videotape to record and analyze science lessons in ten Japanese classrooms and reviewed evidence on Japanese instructional context, curriculum, and policy. They intended to point out differences in context between science education in the United States and Japan and to explore examples of synergies between science instruction and the broader educational system in Japan and implications of such synergies for U.S. efforts in science education reform.

> While definitive conclusions about the nature of Japanese elementary science instruction await large-scale, representative studies, data from the small, convenience samples studied to date suggest that the science activity structures found in Japanese elementary lessons may overlap substantially with those found in many model programs in the United States (Linn et al., 2000:12).

This small-scale international comparative video study provides insight into the relationship between classroom activity structures and larger educational system features. Whether large-scale or small-scale, however, the expense and precision made possible by international videotapes is not necessary for every classroom study.

WHAT VIDEO CAN AND CANNOT CAPTURE

The collection and preservation of video records in computerized archives create many new possibilities for research. TIMSS was one of the first studies to store and manage very large volumes of footage. Researchers can move quickly through digitized videotapes to locate certain events or words. Computerizing the data makes it much easier to store and recall images for future research, and archived tapes serve as a record of teaching as it was done in a particular time and place that can be reexamined at a later point in time.

The benefits of storing videotapes in computerized form would accrue to future scholars. Hiebert argued that video technology produces a less processed form of data than direct observations. A researcher can go back to the footage as many times as necessary to recode what he or she observes, or to search for patterns or events that suggested themselves only after later reflection or a fresh insight. Multiple researchers can work collaboratively on coding and, in the process, begin to understand how different analysis techniques can complement one another. Other scholars could work with the same footage and apply a different coding scheme or attempt to answer a completely different research question than the one that motivated the original data collection. By contrast, a researcher conducting research based on live classroom observations is limited by time; without the possibility of instant replay, he or she has only one opportunity to notice all the myriad events and intricacies of a given lesson. A live observer is also limited by human capabilities: one set of eyes and ears can only focus on a few things at any given moment. In contrast, a video camera records whatever occurs within its frame, and it might take several viewings for an individual observer to take it all in.

Although video technology can clearly capture more than one observer could possibly notice and record, in another sense video technology may capture less. Videographers have options as they decide how to tape a classroom: they might pan across the room or fix on the teacher, depending on the structure and goals of the data collection and the videographer's training. Tapes cannot capture everything that happens in a classroom, and what they miss is typically determined by the position of the camera rather than by a trained observer's instinctive reactions to events as they unfold. Moreover, while video data are less "processed" than other kinds of data, they are not equivalent to direct observational data. The view of someone watching videotape is constricted; he or she is experiencing what is taped through the frame of a host of decisions made before and as the data were collected (Hall, 2000). Ricki Goldman-Segall elaborated on this point by explaining that videographers choose to convey a "story they want to share with [viewers] about what was happening in that place [at] that time."

Culture might affect the framing of videotaped images in international comparative studies. For example, the relationship between a teacher and the students in a classroom is often reciprocal. As David Berliner explained, "The nature of the kids is a very big determinant of what the teachers do." The behaviors of students from different cultures vary in ways that profoundly influence teaching. In examining such differences using video technology, researchers need to consider how student-teacher reciprocity might be captured. A researcher might use two cameras, one to capture the teacher's actions and one to capture the students' behavior. Practical limitations may need to be overcome in recording sound, particularly students talking among themselves. Adding more equipment to record teacher and student behavior and speech might capture more of what is happening, but it might also create more disruption. Depending on the specific goals for the data collection, as well as available resources, researchers should consider the relative benefits and limitations of using cameras that can track or zoom in on particular interactions or respond in other ways to the idiosyncrasies of a particular lesson.

No camera, of course, can record teachers' intentions or students' real-time understanding, reactions, or learning. Moreover, decisions about placing and handling the camera may reflect unconscious assumptions about what will happen during the lesson—an expectation that the teacher will remain in the front of the room, for example—and may indeed subtly influence the actions of teachers or students. These framing decisions are complex in international studies because of cultural, political, and gender-based differences. Heidi Ross and Ricki Goldman-Segall reinforced the message that the complexity of these framing decisions in international video has implications for what viewers see and how they make sense of it. While a variety of factors will undoubtedly influence every research design, the inclusion of contextual material will enhance the usefulness of video data that is archived or intended for use by multiple researchers.

PRIVACY AND CONFIDENTIALITY

Videotapes are easy to share; indeed, many interested in this methodology speak enthusiastically about the possibility of using the Internet as a means of sharing digitized footage that can be used by researchers anywhere for a wide variety of purposes. This possibility leads to the question of obtaining informed consent from the participants of such research. Assuming that anonymity cannot be guaranteed and that the videotapes will be placed in archives, how can researchers protect research participants?

The difficulties surrounding informed consent present immediate and pressing practical obstacles for researchers already involved in international video research projects who must identify statistically sound samples of participants and obtain their cooperation in a fair manner. Issues of privacy are connected to deep cultural meanings and assumptions about public teaching. Several workshop participants spoke about the variability across cultures of ideas about privacy and the social context in which teachers' performance is viewed. The presence of a video camera in the classroom may have a very different meaning for the students, teachers, and administrators in one country than in another. Indeed, the sampling of Japanese classrooms for the TIMSS Videotape Classroom Study was complicated in part by the desire of education officials to put the teachers they considered the very best in the spotlight. In some cultures, teachers might be reluctant to be taped or very uncomfortable in front of the camera, while in others taping might be commonplace. The possible consequences of judgments about teachers' performance will vary by country as well—and likely affect teachers' views about being taped—but disentangling cultural differences from individual variation is often tricky. Government agencies, some of which have faced distrust from citizens because of inappropriate data collection efforts in the past, are now major funders of video research and remain particularly concerned about setting standards for professional conduct in this area.

The public release of the TIMSS videotapes in 1998 offers insight into issues of confidentiality and consent. TIMSS researchers planned to use videotapes to help communicate the results of the study to the general public. However, because the survey participants had been guaranteed confidentiality, the actual survey footage could not be released to the public. Consequently, another set of videos was filmed for use in public discussions at such forums as PTA meetings, professional conferences, and teacher training events. The participants of these tapes provided explicit permission for this dissemination, but as the TIMSS researchers noted: "It is not easy to find teachers who will agree to being videotaped for public viewing" (Stigler et al., 1999:14).

Many of the workshop participants noted that discussions of publicly released videotapes have often focused on the negative and, at times, deteriorated into teacher blaming. John Frederiksen described this tendency toward criticism as "normative negativity." The viewing public focuses on what appears to be wrong in the lessons shown and not on what appears to be working effectively. Participants discussed the TIMSS Videotape Classroom Study as an example of how normative negativity might influence teachers' willingness to allow a video record of their teaching to be made public. A major theme in the discussion of the TIMSS results was the perceived inadequacy of U.S. schools, and of U.S. teachers in particular. As Joseph Tobin summarized, "The study is so thick with the sense of despair about the quality of American math education that, of course, there are a lot of problems of confidentiality especially for the Americans." Public discussions that lead to comparisons between teachers, with some teachers' performance being cited as examples of inferior practice, could also have a chilling effect on teachers.

Because evaluation and judgment have become an almost inevitable aspect in video research on classrooms, the traditional roles of researchers and research participants have been somewhat altered. Tobin, Magdalene Lampert, and others highlighted how video technology as a tool for observation brings some troubling connotations from other contexts. Video cameras are used for surveillance in stores, banks, and even prisons. They are sometimes used by parents to monitor the performance of their children's day care centers or nannies. These uses of video technology all place subjects in a vulnerable position because the observer is in a position to intervene to prevent a bad outcome, and in possession of legal evidence of any actionable wrongdoing. When calls for school accountability often mean a direct connection between test scores and job security for administrators and teachers and when a misunderstood phrase can lead to disciplinary action, it should come as no surprise that videotaping in classrooms seems ominous to some.

Practical solutions for addressing the tension between protecting the privacy of participants, scholarly access, and research need to be developed. For example, facial features might be disguised, although current technology renders doing so difficult for large volumes of tape. Furthermore, important information would surely be lost. Different levels of confidentiality might be guaranteed for videos collected for different purposes, ranging from very strict measures for tapes to be posted on the Internet for general public access, to very limited measures for tapes to which only registered scholars would have access. Permission for broader dissemination may result in lower participation by research participants, with implications for sampling size and representativeness. Lack of informed consent from one or two participants in a large class also creates complications for video data collection.

Restrictions placed on video data by university Institutional Review Boards (IRBs) charged with protecting research participants may also hinder researchers' use of video. In some extreme cases, in the interest of confidentiality, IRBs might require that videos be destroyed rather than archived. Clearly, these issues are very complex and require continuing attention from educators and ethicists, as well as researchers who have used video technology for a variety of purposes, to develop guidelines for the research community. Issues of confidentiality are further complicated in the case of international video because of cross-cultural differences in perceptions about privacy and teaching, as well as by the potential power of international video to reach and affect large and disparate audiences.

PROFESSIONAL DEVELOPMENT

In addition to being a useful methodological tool for research, video technology can also support and improve the practice of teaching. As noted by many workshop participants, videotaped lessons have proven very useful in stimulating conversations about teaching. Videotapes can be used to help teachers to imagine new approaches, to rethink what they might otherwise take for granted, to consider the pros and cons of different approaches, and, in general, to reflect on their practice in new ways.

Videotaped footage from cross-national studies in education is particularly useful for provoking reflections on practice and prompting new ways of envisioning education. Frederick Erickson observed:

> Teaching has been such a secret local practice, that we always assume that what we have figured out how to do is the way it has to be. Seeing something that is really very different from far away can open up the possibility that there are lots of different roads to Rome. That opens up, I think, readiness for inquiry to change that can be very powerful.

He noted that looking at the practice of a teacher from the next classroom can lead to new insights about one's own practice. Looking at the practice of a teacher from another country can cause an even more profound rethinking of assumptions. Erickson's insights focus attention on a question for international comparative education research: How does the effect of viewing a teacher from another culture differ from viewing a teacher from one's own culture?

The potential for international videotapes to stretch people's thinking about familiar topics is only beginning to be explored. Further research into what and how people learn from watching international videos will help guide teacher educators in identifying the best uses of video technology. Workshop participants described the ways in which they have used video to improve teacher professional development to shed light on current practices and understanding. The flexibility of the new technology has clearly inspired considerable creative thinking about what happens in classrooms and, in BICSE's view, has helped focus both the public and the research and policy communities on teaching in a way that seems both novel and constructive. Lampert observed that the TIMSS videos have been influential in helping people see teaching as a process that can be studied and have helped educators isolate some of its component parts: "There is a lot to suggest that teachers don't teach on the basis of what they see happening in their classrooms. They are not reflective practitioners, on the whole." She identified several applications of video technology that have potential for teacher development to help teachers learn and improve through that reflective thinking:

- learning a particular teaching technique;
- using evidence to analyze the relationship between particular teaching and evidence of learning;
- exposing teachers to new ideas, alternatives, or inspiration; and
- using videotapes to discuss and understand variations in teaching practice, to establish a more precise language of teaching that goes beyond simple characterizations of "good" and "bad."

Lampert argued that developing a shared professional language about teaching through the interpretation of video would constitute professional development, ". . . in the sense that it would enable teaching to become more of a practice-based profession."

John Frederiksen also provided insights into using reflection to transform teaching into a practice-based profession. He discussed ways that teachers can improve their cognitive and social skills in the process of viewing and interpreting video data collaboratively. He described a model in which teachers view and interpret classroom video coverage together in order to share and discuss ideas about instructional practices—video clubs. Eventually, the teachers develop a shared set of criteria for evaluating teacher effectiveness in accomplishing instructional goals, such as "mathematical thinking is going on" or "participants in the class are showing mutual respect." Such criteria are not used as a basis for judging appropriate teaching behaviors; "[r]ather, they must facilitate recognizing in a video when teaching moves are meeting particular teaching goals in the particular teaching situations shown in the video," Frederiksen said. By focusing on function, he argued, teachers are better able to concentrate on how instructional goals are being achieved rather than on specific forms of classroom organization or pedagogical strategies. Teachers are thus engaged in the process of reflecting about the practices of others, as well as their own practices, and encouraged to investigate the extent to which they are achieving their own goals.

Frederiksen noted that this reflective process fosters important professional skills, such as an "evaluative judgment" of efficacy and "an inquiry attitude towards classroom teaching, innovation, and changing of one's practice." This model of video interpretation, he argued, can help teachers create a language of practice that directs attention to a broad range of teaching goals and methods for learning. Teachers can view and discuss many styles and situations and encounter practices they can experiment with in their own classrooms. Frederiksen described an example of how video clubs "proved to be a powerful catalyst for improving teaching practice" in his research on video portfolio assessment (Frederiksen et al., 1998:276). A member of one of the clubs gave a video presentation on her use of collaborative groups in mathematics. Her approach was very different from the teacher-centered classrooms that the rest of the video club members used. As a result of this meeting, three members took the initiative to change their teaching styles to incorporate more group work and then shared videotapes of themselves using this approach in subsequent meetings. "These club members were in essence carrying out design experiments . . . in their classrooms, using the video club as a research group to help them interpret the outcomes of their experiments" (Frederiksen et al., 1998:277).

Drew Gitomer said that one of the challenges of cross-national studies is encouraging teachers to see the relevance of classroom practices from another country to their own professional experience. Teachers can easily dismiss research findings if the context of the teaching depicted in a video is very different from their own. High school teachers may consider portrayals of elementary level instruction irrelevant to their own work; teachers in rural schools may not see the relevance of videos from urban districts; and U.S. teachers may see little relevance in videotapes of lessons in Germany or Japan.

Heidi Ross explained the value in using the sometimes radical differences across cultures that are evident in international video research as a catalyst for reflective thinking. She argued for the value of using classroom images from other countries to begin discussions and raise awareness among preservice teachers about the complexity of teaching practice. International video research can help them develop a critical understanding about how they have been socialized and how that socialization will affect what they do in their classrooms once they become teachers. Videotapes of practices in other countries can help U.S. teachers explore cultural values and what is important to them as teachers in comparison with what might be important to teachers in other cultures.

Videotapes can also be used to present models of effective practice for the purpose of asking teachers to model their own practice on it. However, the board believes that using international videotapes to present exemplary practice and train teachers to adopt it is a particularly problematic enterprise that deserves more careful scrutiny than it has received thus far. At least two major drawbacks are evident. First, using videotapes to suggest specific changes in teaching practice is a higher stakes enterprise than simply using videotape as a point of departure for discussion. One of the risks is creating a misconception about a standard that does not take into account other contextual factors affecting teacher practice. Second, identifying the precise elements of teaching that should be imitated is complicated; specifically, it requires the establishment of an empirical link between a particular teaching method or approach and improvements in student learning. International videotape studies have yet to make this link.

LINKS BETWEEN ACHIEVEMENT AND TEACHING PRACTICES

Participants in the workshop agreed that empirical links between specific teacher practices demonstrated in videotaped lessons and learning outcomes have not yet been established. TIMSS serves as an example, since many researchers were interested in linking observations made in the TIMSS Videotape Classroom Study with TIMSS achievement scores. James Stigler explained in his written contribution to the workshop how the design of the TIMSS Videotape Classroom Study "precluded any causal inferences on the relationship between teaching and learning, either at the level of nation or at the level of teacher/class" for several reasons. At the national level, the sample size of countries in the TIMSS videotape study was three, "and the potential causes of achievement differences are many." At the teacher level, researchers videotaped only one lesson per teacher, "which does not give a reliable indication of any particular teacher's practice." Stigler also pointed out that even if multiple lessons by the same teacher were videotaped, this approach measures teaching and achievement at just one point in time and does not account for students' previous learning experiences.

Participants at the workshop differed over whether such links between teaching and learning are likely to be established in the foreseeable future. From BICSE's perspective, resolving these differences would require a large-scale study, incorporating a large sample of teachers and many background variables to capture their diversity. Deep understanding of the classroom interactions studied and the cultural contexts in which the lessons were conducted are just two of the components that would be necessary to make such a link persuasive.

Workshop participants noted several issues that a persuasive study would probably have to address. Some noted that achievement data, at least in the United States, are generally relatively unstable; ideally, multiple measures of achievement should be used to establish valid links to instructional practice. One might videotape teachers teaching a single common lesson in various ways and compare the learning outcomes. Other participants, however, suggested that it would be difficult to distinguish the learning attributable to teacher practice from the learning attributable to previous learning, motivation, and other factors students bring to the classroom.

While some participants argued that being able to characterize the achievement outcomes of the teaching that is taped is critical to making use of the observations, others noted that the link itself may be a misleading goal. For Joseph Tobin, for example, the comparison of achievement scores may have little relevance to the insights about teaching he would seek from comparative videos since variations in learning have so many other sources. Catherine Lewis seconded that view, noting that "whatever it is that's causing achievement may not be represented in videos" and that deep ethnographic descriptions are necessary to ascertain the ingredients for learning in a particular setting. Ray McDermott noted that a focus on achievement should include how different countries define achievement, given different cultural contexts. The Japanese definition of achievement might be very different from the U.S. definition, so it is important to examine the cultural organization of what achievement is in cross-national comparative studies in education. Other participants suggested that cross-national video studies might best be used to *generate* hypotheses about effects of teaching on learning, while large-scale video studies within countries might be better suited to *testing* the hypotheses that are generated through cross-national comparisons.

CONCLUSIONS AND RECOMMENDATIONS

The Board on International Comparative Studies in Education concludes that international videotapes of students and teaching are a powerful tool for learning about and improving education. Videotapes of classrooms in other countries are particularly powerful in creating opportunities for learning from cross-national and cross-cultural comparisons. Video images of educational settings from around the world stimulate reflection and expand understanding of the potential range of instructional practices.

Despite its novelty and its power to capture attention, however, this technology is a tool, not an end in itself. Researchers continue to grapple with complex questions regarding both the methodology and practical applications of this tool. Many such questions are not yet resolved, among them:

- How feasible will it be for future researchers to return to archived videotapes and recode them according to new schemes?
- How will the privacy of research participants be protected?
- What are the possibilities for using videotape data to link achievement to instructional practices?

BICSE offers four recommendations to guide researchers, funding agencies, and policy makers in the judicious application of video technology as a tool for future international comparative studies.

Recommendation 1: The international comparative education research community should pursue projects that appropriately use video technology as a research tool.

Such research will help scholars build a body of work that can contribute fundamental new understandings of educational practices, while at the same time resolving some of the important methodological challenges discussed in this report.

Recommendation 2: The international comparative education research community should support not only large-scale studies that make use of video technology, such as TIMSS, but also other kinds of video-based research.

Research studies with a variety of sizes, goals, and methodologies can benefit from the application of video technology in important ways that have the potential to stimulate progress in both methodological and substantive issues.

Recommendation 3: The international comparative education research community should undertake initiatives, such as the support of a working group, to help clarify and develop solutions to the privacy and confidentiality issues in using video technology in such research.

The very nature of video technology creates problems for and challenges to confidentiality that cannot be easily handled by simple extrapolation from existing procedures for other research methods. Thus, serious and focused consideration of confidentiality issues in video research, especially in international settings, is needed to develop creative solutions and to foster discussion and consensus building around such solutions.

Recommendation 4: The international comparative education research community should undertake initiatives, such as the support of a working group, to explore the creation of a video archive or archives for international comparative research in education.

Video technology can be of significant benefit in expanding the accessibility and application of comparative research and in serving as a unique historical resource. Given the substantial costs associated with both international comparative education research and video technology, wide distribution and archiving will contribute to its cost effectiveness.

The board hopes that this powerful technology will continue to be harnessed for research that informs international comparative understanding of education. The board sees a bright future for research that capitalizes on the strengths of this important tool while working within its limitations.

REFERENCES

Bateson, G., and M. Mead
    1952 *Bathing Babies in Three Cultures*. Videocassette. University Park, PA: Pennsylvania State University Audiovisual Services.

Bogdan, R., and S. Biklen
    1992 *Qualitative Research for Education: An Introduction to Theory and Methods*. 2nd ed. Boston, MA: Allyn and Bacon.

Campbell, D.
    1961 The mutual methodological relevance of anthropology and psychology. In F. Hsu, ed., *Psychological Anthropology: Approaches to Culture and Personality* (pp. 333-352). Homewood, IL: The Dorsey Press, Inc.

de Brigard, E.
    1995 The history of ethnographic film. In P. Hockings, ed., *Principles of Visual Anthropology*. 2nd ed. (pp. 13-43). New York: Mouton de Gruyter.

Erickson, F.
    1986 Qualitative methods in research on teaching. In M. Wittrock, ed., *Handbook of Research on Teaching*. 3rd ed. (pp. 119-161). New York, NY: MacMillan Publishing Company.
    1992 Ethnographic microanalysis of interaction. In M. LeCompte, W. Millroy, and J. Preissle, eds., *The Handbook of Qualitative Research in Education* (pp. 201-225). New York, NY: Academic Press/Harcourt Brace.

Frederiksen, J., M. Sipusic, M. Sherin, and E. Wolfe
    1998 Video portfolio assessment: Creating a framework for viewing the functions of teaching. *Educational Assessment* 5(4):225-297.

Goldman-Segall, R.
    1998 *Points of Viewing Children's Thinking: A Digital Ethnographer's Journey*. Mahwah, NJ: Lawrence Erlbaum Associates.

Hall, R.
    2000 Videorecording as theory. In A.E. Kelly and R.A. Lesh, eds., *Handbook of Research Design in Mathematics and Science Education* (pp. 647-664). Mahwah, NJ: Lawrence Erlbaum Associates.

Henley, P.
    1998 Film-making and ethnographic research. In J. Prosser, ed., *Image-based Research: A Sourcebook for Qualitative Researchers* (pp. 42-59). Bristol, PA: Falmer Press, Taylor & Francis, Inc.

Jordan, B., and A. Henderson
    1995 Interaction analysis: Foundations and practice. *The Journal of the Learning Sciences* 4(1):39-103.

Linn, M., C. Lewis, I. Tsuchida, and N. Songer
    2000 Beyond fourth-grade science: Why do U.S. and Japanese students diverge? *Educational Researcher* 29(3):4-14.

McDermott, R., and D. Roth
    1978 The social organization of behavior: Interactional approaches. *Annual Review of Anthropology* 7:321-345.

National Research Council
- 1999 *Next Steps for TIMSS: Directions for Secondary Analysis.* Board on International Comparative Studies in Education, A. Beatty, L.W. Paine, and F.O. Ramirez, eds. Board on Testing and Assessment. Commission on Behavioral and Social Sciences and Education. Washington, DC: National Academy Press.

Spindler, G., and L. Spindler
- 1992 Cultural process and ethnography: an anthropological perspective. In M. LeCompte, W. Millroy, and J. Preissle, eds., *The Handbook of Qualitative Research in Education* (pp. 53-92). New York, NY: Academic Press/Harcourt Brace.

Stigler, J., R. Gallimore, and J. Hiebert
- 2000 Using video surveys to compare classrooms and teaching across cultures: Examples and lessons from the TIMSS video studies. *Educational Psychologist* 35(2):87-100.

Stigler, J., P. Gonzales, T. Kawanaka, S. Knoll, and A. Serrano
- 1999 *The TIMSS Videotape Classroom Study: Methods and Findings from an Exploratory Research Project on Eighth-Grade Mathematics Instruction in Germany, Japan, and the United States.* National Center for Education Statistics. Washington, DC: U.S. Department of Education.

Taft, L.
- 1985 Ethnographic research methods. In T. Husen and T. Postlethwaite, eds., *The International Encyclopedia of Education: Research and Studies* (Vol. 3, pp. 1729-1733). New York: Pergamon Press.

Tobin, J., D. Wu, and D. Davidson
- 1989 *Preschool in Three Cultures: Japan, China, and the United States.* New Haven, CT: Yale University Press.

Appendix
Workshop Agenda and Participants

The Uses of Video in International Education Studies: A Workshop

AGENDA
November 30, 1999

National Academy of Sciences Building
2101 Constitution Avenue
Lecture Room
8:00 a.m.-4:45 p.m.

8:00-8:30	*Continental breakfast in meeting room*
8:30-9:30	Welcome and introductions Overview of BICSE's mission Andrew Porter, BICSE chair Goals for the workshop and introduction of expert participants Clea Fernandez, Lynn Paine, Janet Schofield
9:30-12:45	**Panel Discussions**
9:30-11:00	***Use #1:*** ***Descriptions of classroom practice across countries*** James Hiebert, University of Delaware Catherine Lewis, Mills College Frederick Erickson, University of California, Los Angeles Discussion Leader: Joseph Tobin, University of Hawaii at Manoa
11:00-11:15	*Break*

11:15-12:45	***Use #2:*** ***Supporting professional development and improving practice*** John Frederiksen, Educational Testing Service Drew Gitomer, Educational Testing Service Ricki Goldman-Segall, MERLin, University of British Columbia Heidi Ross, Colgate University Discussion Leader: Magdalene Lampert, University of Michigan
12:45-1:30	*Lunch in meeting room*
1:30-2:45	**Panel discussions continued**
1:30-2:45	***Use #3:*** ***Understanding achievement differences within and across countries*** David Berliner, BICSE member James Stigler, University of California, Los Angeles Discussion Leader: Raymond McDermott, Stanford University
2:45-3:00	*Break*
3:00-4:00	**Moderated discussion** • What are the most fruitful purposes for the use of video in international studies? Which purposes seem less worthwhile? • What are the biggest challenges for the use of video in international studies? • What unique opportunities are provided by the use of video in international studies? Discussants: Magdalene Lampert, Raymond McDermott, Joseph Tobin Moderators: Clea Fernandez, Lynn Paine, Janet Schofield
4:00-4:30	Final thoughts from invited experts
4:30-4:45	Summary remarks Andrew Porter
4:45	Adjourn

PARTICIPANTS

Jennifer Adams, Graduate School of Education, Harvard University
Gordon M. Ambach,* Council of Chief State School Officers, Washington, D.C.
Ronald Anderson, Department of Sociology, University of Minnesota
Sousan Arafeh, Education Statistics Services Institute, American Institutes for Research
Alexandra Beatty, Board on Testing and Assessment, National Research Council
David C. Berliner,* College of Education, Arizona State University
Chris Calsyn, Education Statistics Services Institute, American Institutes for Research
Christopher T. Cross,* Council for Basic Education, Washington, D.C.
John A. Dossey,* Department of Mathematics, Illinois State University
Janice Earle, Division of Elementary, Secondary, and Informal Education, National Science Foundation
Frederick Erickson, Graduate School of Education and Information Studies, University of California Los Angeles
John Frederiksen, Cognitive Science Research Group, Educational Testing Service, Oakland, California
Adam Gamoran,* Departments of Sociology and Educational Policy Studies, University of Wisconsin-Madison
Drew Gitomer, Vice President of Research, Educational Testing Service, Princeton, New Jersey
Ricki Goldman-Segall, Multimedia Ethnographic Research Lab, Faculty of Education, University of British Columbia
Patrick Gonzales, National Center for Education Statistics, U.S. Department of Education
James Hiebert, School of Education, University of Delaware
Eamonn Kelly, Division of Research on Education, Policy and Practice, National Science Foundation
Robert Kozma, Center for Technology in Learning, SRI International
Magdalene Lampert, School of Education, University of Michigan
Laurence Lanahan, Education Statistics Services Institute, American Institutes for Research
Mariann Lemke, Planning and Evaluation Service, U.S. Department of Education
Catherine Lewis, Developmental Studies Center, Education Department, Mills College, Oakland, California
Marlaine E. Lockheed,* The World Bank, Washington, D.C.
Raymond McDermott, School of Education, Stanford University

Daniel McGrath, Education Statistics Services Institute, American Institutes for Research

Patricia Morison, Board on International Comparative Studies in Education, National Research Council

Lynn W. Paine,* Department of Teacher Education, Michigan State University

Jane Phillips, Board on International Comparative Studies in Education, National Research Council

Andrew C. Porter,* Wisconsin Center for Educational Research, University of Wisconsin-Madison

Heidi Ross, Education Department, Colgate University

Laura Salganik, Education Statistics Services Institute, American Institutes for Research

Janet Ward Schofield,* Learning Research and Development Center, University of Pittsburgh

Ramsay Selden, Education Statistics Services Institute, American Institutes for Research

Larry Suter, Division of Research on Education, Policy and Practice, National Science Foundation

Joseph Tobin, College of Education, University of Hawaii at Manoa

Elizabeth VanderPutten, Division of Research on Education, Policy and Practice, National Science Foundation

---

*Member of BICSE in 1999.